the soy sauce cookbook

the SOY
cookbook

Explore the flavour-enhancing
power of Asia's magic
ingredient

by Jenny Stacey and
Maureen Keller

TED SMART

A QUINTET BOOK

This edition produced for
The Book People Ltd
Hall Wood Avenue
Haydock
St Helens WA I I 9UL

ISBN 1-85613-736-8
This book was designed and produced by
Quintet Publishing Limited
6 Blundell Street
London N7 9BH

creative director: **Richard Dewing**
art director: **Clare Reynolds**
design: **Balley Design Associates**
designers: **Simon Balley & Joanna Hill**
project editor: **Doreen Palamartschuk**
editor: **Jane Hurd-Cosgrave**
photographer: **David Armstrong**

Typeset in Great Britain by
Central Southern Typesetters, Eastbourne
Manufactured in Singapore by
United Graphic Pte Ltd
Printed in Singapore by
Star Standard Industries Pte Ltd
Photographs on pages 6(tl), 7, 8(bl), and 9(tr)
courtesy of Kikkoman Soy Sauce.

above: **A traditional soy sauce ceramic jar.**

below: **Dark soy sauce.**

Known as *Shoyu* or "fermented savoury agent" in Japan and *jiang yong* in China, soy sauce is as indispensable to cooks and chefs in China and Japan as salt, pepper and mustard are elsewhere. It is an essential component of all Oriental cooking. Every table hosts a bottle of light or dark soy sauce at all mealtimes to be used as a seasoning or dip.

We still associate soy sauce with Oriental recipes and cooking methods, and do not use it to its full potential. In fact, soy sauce is a healthy, versatile ingredient that can be used as a basis for rich sauces, soups, dips, marinades and salad dressings, or simply drizzled over roast or fried dishes, enhancing everything it touches with its uniquely piquant flavour.

light and dark soy sauce

Although there are a few variations with additional ingredients for added flavour, the two main types of soy sauce are the light and the dark varieties. These are each very distinctive, and each blends best with different types of food.

Light soy sauce, as the name implies, is light in colour and less powerful in flavour, although the flavour remains full. It is more widely used for sauces, and is the most suitable for use in cooking. Saltier than dark soy sauce, it is known in Chinese stores as Superior Soy, and is mainly used in soups or with fish, seafood, light meats and poultry.

Dark soy sauce is matured for a longer period than light soy, which causes its dark, almost-black appearance. Slightly thicker than light soy, it has a stronger, sweeter flavour, and is more suitable for stews, casseroles and recipes with dark meats. It is also used when a dipping sauce consisting only of soy sauce is called for. It is known to Chinese grocers as Soy Superior Sauce.

what is soy sauce?

Called "liquid spice", naturally brewed soy sauce contains more than 280 aromatic ingredients, including vanilla extract, fruits, flowers, meat, fish and alcohol, which enable it to enhance many dishes with its subtle fragrance. Based on soy beans, wheat, water, salt and a specially developed yeast, soy sauce is brewed in a similar fashion to a fine wine. Other ingredients are added according to the origin of the sauce. Pork is added in Canton; ginger and mushrooms are added in Peking; occasionally, anchovy paste is also added. Naturally brewed soy sauce is free from additives and preservatives. There are, however, other less natural processes that are used to produce soy sauce chemically. These are considered to be inferior in aroma and flavour by true soy sauce connoisseurs.

above: **The Imperial Soy Sauce Museum, Goyogura, Japan.**

the history of soy sauce

Japanese soy sauce was first introduced to the West by Dutch explorers in the 17th century. It was they who introduced it to Europe, exporting it in stone jars and barrels. Soy sauce soon became popular in France, where Louis XIV's royal chefs discovered its uses as a flavour enhancer.

The Chinese, however, were the original users of soy sauce. They introduced it to Japan, along with the influence of Buddhism, over 1,500 years ago. The Buddhist religion forbade the use of meat and fish-based sauces, which traditionally played a great part in flavouring foods. Soy sauce soon became a popular seasoning in Japan, although it was changed from its original form: it was originally made only from soy beans and the Japanese version had wheat added to it.

how soy sauce is produced

Naturally brewed soy sauce is produced when soy beans and wheat are mixed together to form a dry mash known as "koji". The koji mixture grows over a period of 45 hours, during which time special enzymes that are vital to the sauce's final flavour, colour and aroma begin to form. Next, a salt water solution is added and the mixture is then left to ferment for up to six months. The resulting mixture is known as a "mature

below: **Ancient Japanese soy sauce production drawing.**

above: **Light soy sauce.**

mash", and resembles a smooth, reddish-brown liquid. The mash is then pressed between layers of cloth to extract the clear soy sauce, which is then pasteurized and bottled.

A good soy sauce has 280 different flavour and aroma components. These blend in such a way that no single flavour dominates, resulting in a product that may be used with a wide variety of ingredients. There are three methods of producing soy sauce, and the end products vary in quality and flavour: one type of fermented or brewed soy sauce is produced by fermenting the soy beans, wheat, water and salt with no further additions. This type is completely natural.

A non-brewed sauce is chemically produced by hydrolysing plant protein, which is then blended with colourings, salt water, corn syrup and caramel.

A semi-brewed soy sauce is also produced by combining the two previous methods together. Artificial or chemically produced soy sauce is made when the vegetable or plant proteins are decomposed at a high temperature by the addition of powerful acids, such as hydrochloric acid. This mixture is then neutralized with the addition of soda. The final additions are HVP (hydrolysed vegetable protein), sugar, salt and caramel. The final product is considered to be lacking in flavour and aroma when compared to naturally brewed soy sauces, such as Japanese brands.

below: **Drawing of Japanese soy sauce production.**

Chinese-style soy sauce is different again. This ferments in just 30 days. The lack of yeast gives a fermentation that is low in alcohol and lactic acids and a resultant sauce that some people say lacks flavour and aroma.

Japanese-style, naturally brewed soy sauce is made by traditional methods that have been handed down for 350 years. The soy beans are first steamed and then mixed with equal proportions of roasted, crushed-wheat kernels. Yeast is then added to start the natural fermentation process. After three days, the soy and wheat germ mixture grows a mould over the surface, at which stage it is known as

"koji". This mixture is blended with salted water and the resulting wet mash put into fermentation tanks.

Over a period of weeks, the soy bean protein changes to amino acids, which give the final sauce its characteristic taste. Wheat starch changes to sugar and the mixture of this and the acids forms the colour of the sauce. The sugar content gradually changes to alcohol and some of the alcohol and sugar transforms into various acids which add tartness to the flavour. This mixture matures for six months and is then pressed. The liquid, which is the soy sauce, is then drawn off, pasteurized and bottled.

above: **Soy fermenting in chrysanthemum-wood vats.**

soy sauce today

You can see from these different processes that there are different qualities of soy sauce on the market today. If possible, try to use the naturally brewed sauces in your cooking to give a fuller flavour.

There is an ancient taste test that is said to distinguish between a good sauce and a lesser sauce. A good sauce can be enjoyed on its own when poured into a dish, but a lesser sauce will be too harsh and unpleasant if taken in this way.

below: **A modern collection of soy sauce bottles.**

Soy sauce was initially used as a seasoning by the Chinese to complement their vegetarian diet; now, it is also used in stewed dishes and marinades in China and as a table condiment in Indonesia. It may be used in many types of cooking, not all of them Oriental, and with many ingredients. The addition of soy sauce gives a spicy, salty flavour to dishes, without overpowering them. Soy sauce is generally used in small quantities, as you will see from the following recipes.

Another advantage of soy sauce as a condiment and flavour-enhancer is that it has an indefinite shelf life if stored correctly, and so does not need to be used quickly. Store the sauce as you would a fine wine, with its cap firmly sealed and keep it in the refrigerator or a cool place to prevent it from oxidizing. Once you begin to realize the full potential of soy sauce by trying the delicious recipes featured in this book, long storage will not be an issue you will have to consider. So get out the soy sauce and enter a whole new world of tastes!

savoury
snacks

Curried Parcels

Easy to prepare, these parcels may be served hot or cold, perhaps with a mint and yoghurt dip to complement the Indian flavours in the filling.

serves 4

75 g/3 oz prepared puff pastry, thawed	I tsp garam masala
I egg, beaten	½ tsp chilli powder
I tsp sesame seeds	I Tbsp peach chutney
	2 tsp lemon juice
	I small carrot, finely
for the filling	diced
I Tbsp butter	I Tbsp light soy sauce
2 spring onions, chopped	120 g/4 oz diced,
2 garlic cloves, crushed	cooked potato

Melt the butter for the filling and gently cook the spring onions, garlic, garam masala, chilli, chutney, lemon juice, carrot and soy sauce, stirring for 3 to 4 minutes. Add the potato, mix well and leave to cool completely.

Heat the oven to 200°C/400°F/Gas mark 6. Roll the pastry out into a 22 cm/8 in square. Cut into four 10 cm/4 in squares. Brush the edges of the squares with beaten egg and place a little filling in the centre of each square. Carefully draw the corners to the centre to form a parcel, sealing the seams by pressing gently together. Repeat with all of the squares.

Place the parcels on a dampened baking tray, brush with beaten egg and sprinkle with the sesame seeds. Bake in the oven until golden, about 15 minutes.

Stuffed Mushrooms

Capers, feta cheese and soy sauce give these stuffed mushrooms a Middle Eastern flavour.

makes 14 to 16 mushrooms	
350 g/12 oz large mushrooms (14 to 16)	½ tsp olive oil (plus oil for brushing the mushrooms)
25 g/1 oz crumbled feta cheese	1 tsp light soy sauce
25 g/1 oz Italian-style breadcrumbs	½ tsp ground thyme
	1 tsp grated onion
	3 tsp capers, drained

Wash the mushrooms and remove the stems. Chop the stems very finely and place in a bowl. Add 3 tablespoons of the cheese, together with the breadcrumbs and mix thoroughly. Stir in the olive oil and soy sauce. When well blended, stir in the thyme, grated onion and drained capers.

Brush the mushroom caps with olive oil, inside and out. Stuff with the breadcrumb mixture. Then crumble the remaining tablespoon of feta over the mushrooms. Grill until heated thoroughl, and the tops begin to brown, about 6 to 8 minutes.

Spicy Peanuts

Plain peanuts make a good starter, but spicy peanuts are even better. Use a hot curry powder and serve them with lots of beer.

makes 450 g/1 lb

1 Tbsp olive oil	1 Tbsp light soy sauce
2 large garlic cloves, crushed	1 Tbsp Worcestershire sauce
450 g/1 lb roasted, unsalted peanuts	1 tsp curry powder

Heat the olive oil in a pan and add the garlic, stirring. Add the peanuts, soy sauce, Worcestershire sauce and curry powder. Sauté for a few minutes until the liquid has been absorbed. Remove peanuts from the heat and cool before serving.

Hot and Spicy Chicken Wings

A real favourite for supper, these chicken wings are also perfect for barbecues.

serves 4

1 kg/2 lb chicken wings	2 Tbsp dark soy sauce
2 Tbsp garlic wine vinegar	A few drops of Tabasco sauce
2 Tbsp honey	1 Tbsp tomato purée
1 Tbsp Worcestershire sauce	175 ml/6 fl oz passata
	1 tsp prepared mustard

Heat the oven to 180°C/350°F/Gas mark 5. Place the chicken wings in a shallow, ovenproof dish. Place the vinegar, honey, Worcestershire sauce, soy sauce, Tabasco sauce, tomato purée, tomatoes, and mustard in a bowl. Mix well. Pour over the chicken wings, turning to coat evenly.

Cook the chicken wings in the oven until cooked through, about 45 minutes. Serve hot with salad.

Fried Prawn Rolls

Oriental in flavour these prawn-filled bites are delicious, with a hint of coconut and lime to complement the fish. Prepare in advance, then store in the refrigerator so they will be ready to cook just before serving.

serves 4

4 thick slices white bread, with crusts removed	Oil for deep frying
1 Tbsp butter, softened	50 g/2 oz fresh, brown breadcrumbs
1 Tbsp plain flour	1 Tbsp sesame seeds
2 Tbsp coconut milk	1 egg, beaten
1 Tbsp light soy sauce	for the dip
1 Tbsp Romano cheese, grated	150 ml/¼ pt yoghurt
Grated rind of 1 lime	150 ml/¼ pt mayonnaise
75 g/3 oz peeled, cooked prawns, chopped	1 tsp fish sauce
2 spring onions, finely chopped	1 Tbsp tomato purée
Ground black pepper	1 tsp lime juice
	1 Tbsp chopped fresh parsley

Using a rolling pin, flatten the bread slices until very thin. Melt the butter in a pan, add the flour and mix well. Cook for 1 minute, then add the coconut milk and bring to the boil, stirring. Remove the pan from the heat and stir in the soy sauce, cheese, lime rind, prawns and spring onions. Season with pepper.

Spread the mixture on to the bread, roll up, and cut each slice into four. Mix the ingredients for the dip, and chill until required.

Heat the oil in a wok or frying pan to 190°C/370°F. Meanwhile, mix the breadcrumbs and sesame seeds together in a bowl. Then place the beaten egg in a separate bowl. Dip each piece into the egg and then roll in the bread-crumb mixture to coat completely. Fry in the hot oil for 3 minutes. Drain on kitchen paper to remove excess oil and serve with the dip.

Sesame Pikelets

Pikelets are a traditional form of pancake. Make the batter just before cooking.
It is thicker than normal pancake batter in order to hold its shape in the pan.

serves 4

for the pikelets
100 g/4 oz self-raising
flour
1 tsp sesame seeds
2 Tbsp butter, melted
(plus extra for
frying)

150 ml/¼ pt milk
1 Tbsp light soy sauce

for the topping
225 g/8 oz smoked
salmon fillets
2 Tbsp snipped, fresh
chives

1 Tbsp chopped dill
150 ml/¼ pt soured
cream
Lemon wedges

Sieve the flour into a large mixing bowl. Add the sesame seeds and make
a well in the centre, gradually whisking in the butter, milk and soy sauce.

Grease a large, heavy based frying pan or wok with butter. Drop 2
tablespoons of mixture into the pan for each pikelet, cooking two at a
time. Cook until the surface of the pikelet bubbles, then turn them until
each side is browned, about 2 to 3 minutes. Cool on a rack. Repeat until
all the mixture is used.

Slice the smoked salmon. Mix half of the herbs into the soured cream.
Spoon the soured cream onto the pikelets, top with the salmon and
sprinkle on remaining herbs. Serve with lemon wedges and a small salad.

Hot and Sour Prawn Soup

This really is a colourful soup in all aspects. Filled with prawns and vegetables,
it has a truly unique flavour.

serves 4

4 dried Chinese mushrooms

900 ml/1 ½ pt vegetable stock

175 g/6 oz peeled cooked prawns

75 g/3 oz sliced pickled Chinese vegetables

50 g/2 oz canned bamboo shoots, drained and sliced

3 spring onions, sliced

1 courgette, grated

1 cm/½ in piece fresh root ginger, grated

2 tomatoes, seeded and diced

2 tsp rice wine or sherry

2 Tbsp light soy sauce

1 Tbsp red wine vinegar

2 Tbsp smoked ham, diced

1 tsp sesame oil

Soak the dried mushrooms in warm water for 20 minutes. Squeeze dry,
remove the stems and slice. Bring the stock to the boil in a large saucepan.
Add the prawns, vegetables, bamboo shoots, spring onions, courgette,
ginger and tomatoes. Simmer for 5 minutes.

Add the rice wine or sherry, soy sauce, vinegar and ham. Cook for 1
minute, then stir in the sesame oil. Serve immediately.

Marinated Mushroom Caps

These tasty mushrooms get better the longer they marinate. They are delicious
whole, but can also be sliced and added to liven up salads.

serves 6

25 g/8 oz button mushrooms

2 Tbsp light soy sauce

60 ml/2 fl oz red wine

(Merlot is recommended)

2 Tbsp red wine vinegar

1 Tbsp sugar

Remove and discard stems from the mushrooms. Wash the caps and pat
them dry. Place the caps in a bowl or jar with a tight lid. Mix the soy
sauce, wine, vinegar and sugar together. Pour over the mushroom caps.

Marinate the mushrooms in the refrigerator at least overnight or up to
three days, turning occasionally. Serve in a bowl with cocktail sticks.

Vegetable Beignets

Crisp vegetables fried in a light batter, which lets the true colours of the vegetables be seen, make an attractive and delicious starter.

serves 4

350 g/12 oz mixed vegetables, such as asparagus spears, peppers, mangetout, cauliflower and broccoli
Oil for deep frying

for the sauce
1 red chilli, chopped
4 Tbsp light soy sauce
4 Tbsp vermouth
75 ml/3 fl oz passata

50 ml/2 fl oz vegetable stock
1 Tbsp soft brown sugar

for the batter
1 egg
150 ml/¼ pt water
1 Tbsp light soy sauce
100 g/4 oz plain flour
50 g/2 oz cornflour
Pinch of salt

Blanch the vegetables for 3 minutes, drain well and pat dry with kitchen paper. Mix the sauce ingredients together. Place in a small pan and heat gently until the sugar dissolves. Keep warm.

Beat the egg, water and soy sauce for the batter. Sieve the flour, cornflour and salt into a bowl. Make a well in the centre and gradually whisk in the egg mixture to form a smooth batter.

Heat the oil to 190°C/370°F in a wok. Dip the vegetables into the batter, then deep-fry in the oil for 2 to 3 minutes. Remove with a slotted spoon and drain on kitchen paper. Serve with the dipping sauce.

Pork Spareribs

These delicious ribs are cooked in a wok with a spicy barbecue sauce.

serves 4	
675 g/1½ lb pork spareribs, cut into 5 cm/2 in pieces	1 tsp ground ginger
	2 garlic cloves, crushed
	¼ tsp Chinese five spice powder
2 Tbsp vegetable oil	
3 Tbsp dark soy sauce	3 Tbsp red wine vinegar
3 Tbsp honey	
2 Tbsp Worcestershire sauce	75 g/3 oz soft dark brown sugar
175 ml/6 fl oz passata	2 Tbsp lime juice

Prepare the ribs and heat the oil in a wok. Add the ribs and cook until brown, about 5 minutes. Reduce heat and cook for a further 10 minutes. Place all the remaining ingredients in a saucepan and heat gently to dissolve the sugar.

Pour the sauce into the wok with the ribs. Cover and cook until the ribs are cooked well through, about 30 minutes. Serve immediately.

Country Pâté

This pâté is lighter than most meat pâtés since it is made with chicken and pork.

serves 8	
300 g/10 oz chicken breast, minced	2 garlic cloves, crushed
	1 tsp cumin seeds
225 g/8 oz pork belly, minced	2 tsp mixed peppercorns
175 g/6 oz smoked bacon, finely diced	5 Tbsp brandy
	2 Tbsp light soy sauce
½ tsp salt	Hot toast or bread, to serve
½ tsp ground nutmeg	

Lightly grease a 900 g/2 lb loaf tin. Place the chicken, pork and bacon in a large mixing bowl. Add the salt, nutmeg, garlic and cumin. Crush the peppercorns and add to the mixture with the brandy and soy sauce. Mix very well, cover and leave to sit for at least 1 hour.

Heat the oven to 150°C/300°F/Gas mark 2. Spoon the mixture into the loaf tin, pressing down well. Place in a roasting tin half filled with hot water. Cook the pâté in the oven about 1½ to 1¾ hours. Remove from the water and leave to cool. Unmould the pâté, slice and serve with hot toast or bread.

Salmon Pâté

This is a really speedy, yet delicious starter. Once the fish is cooked, all the ingredients are simply blended in a food processor. For extra speed, use tinned salmon.

serves 4	
225 g/8 oz salmon fillet	1 Tbsp lemon juice
100 g/4 oz cream cheese	1 Tbsp capers
1 Tbsp light soy sauce	Ground black pepper
1 Tbsp chopped fresh dill	½ tsp paprika
1 Tbsp chopped fresh parsley	Dill sprigs and lemon slices, to garnish
	Hot toast triangles, to serve

Poach the salmon fillets in a large shallow pan for 8 to 10 minutes or until cooked through. Remove from the pan, drain and skin the fish. Chop the fish into pieces and leave to cool completely.

Place the cream cheese, soy sauce, dill, parsley, lemon juice, capers, pepper and cooked salmon in a food processor, and blend 15 seconds.

Transfer to four individual serving ramekins or small dishes. Sprinkle with paprika and chill until required. Garnish with the dill and lemon and serve with hot toast triangles.

poultry
with pizzazz

Honeyed Chicken Breasts

This honey and ginger sauce has a wonderful taste and aroma, and complements the poultry perfectly. Try using turkey as a substitute for chicken for an equally delicious dish.

serves 4

1 Tbsp vegetable oil	4 Tbsp honey
2 Tbsp butter	250 ml/8 fl oz chicken stock
4 chicken breasts, boned	2 Tbsp light soy sauce
1 garlic clove, crushed	3 pieces bottled stem ginger, sliced
2 leeks, sliced	2 Tbsp syrup from bottled ginger
1 red pepper, cut into strips	2 Tbsp garlic wine vinegar
50 g/2 oz baby corn cobs, halved lengthways	2 Tbsp cornflour
2 Tbsp soft brown sugar	

Heat the oil and butter in a frying pan or wok until the butter has melted. Add the chicken and cook for 5 minutes, turning. Add the garlic and leeks and cook for a further 3 minutes. Stir in the red pepper, baby corn, sugar, honey, stock, soy sauce, stem ginger, ginger syrup and vinegar.

Reduce the heat to a simmer and cook until the chicken is cooked well through, about 20 minutes. Blend the cornflour with 4 tablespoons of cold water and stir into the pan. Bring to the boil and cook until the sauce is thickened and clear. Cook for a further 2 minutes and serve.

Chicken in Black Bean Sauce

This sauce is easy to make and far superior to the bottled sauce you can buy.

serves 4

250 ml/8 fl oz vegetable oil	6 spring onions, chopped
	50 g/2 oz mangetout
350 g/12 oz boneless chicken breast, cut into strips	2 Tbsp canned black beans, washed
100 g/4 oz oyster mushrooms	1 cm/½ in piece fresh root ginger, grated
1 small yellow pepper, diced	1 garlic clove, crushed
	2 Tbsp sherry
1 small green pepper, diced	1 cup chicken stock
	2 Tbsp light soy sauce
	2 Tbsp cornflour

Heat the oil in a wok and cook the chicken for 3 minutes. Using a slotted spoon, remove the chicken from the oil and drain on kitchen paper. Pour the oil from the wok, leaving 3 tablespoons. Add the mushrooms, peppers, spring onions and mangetout to the wok and stir-fry for 3 minutes.

Mash the black beans with the ginger, garlic and sherry in a bowl. Add to the wok and then stir in the chicken stock and soy sauce. Cook for 3 minutes. Blend the cornflour with 4 tablespoons of cold water to make a paste and then stir into the wok. Bring to the boil, add the chicken and cook for 5 minutes, stirring. Serve.

Chicken with Mustard Sauce

Wholegrain mustard is used here for a strong flavour with added texture.

serves 4

1 Tbsp vegetable oil	300 g/10 oz open cap mushrooms, sliced
2 garlic cloves, crushed	
450 g/1 lb chicken breast, boned and skinned	2 Tbsp wholegrain mustard
1 fennel bulb, trimmed	3 Tbsp chopped fresh chives
2 Tbsp light soy sauce	
50 g/2 oz butter	Salt and ground black pepper
150 ml/¼ pt double cream	

Heat the oil in a large frying pan or wok and cook the garlic for 1 minute. Cut the chicken into 2.5 cm/1 in cubes, add to the pan and cook for 2 to 3 minutes, stirring. Add the sliced fennel, soy sauce and butter, and stir-fry for 5 minutes. Stir in the cream, mushrooms, and mustard and cook for 5 minutes. Sprinkle with chopped chives. Season and serve.

Chinese Cashew Casserole

Soy sauce is excellent in casseroles, its piquancy adding a hint of the Orient to this cashew nut and chicken dish.

s e r v e s   4

2 Tbsp sunflower oil
4 chicken pieces
8 shallots
225 g/8 oz chestnut
mushrooms,
quartered
100 g/4 oz baby turnips
2 celery stalks, sliced
1 carrot, diced
25 g/1 oz plain flour
600 ml/1 pt chicken
stock
2 Tbsp light soy sauce

150 ml/¼ pt dry white
wine
50 g/2 oz unsalted
cashew nuts
1 Tbsp tomato purée
Salt and ground black
pepper

for the
dumplings
100 g/ 4 oz self-raising
flour
50 g/2 oz shredded beef
suet

1 Tbsp light soy sauce
1 Tbsp chopped fresh
rosemary

Heat the oil in a large frying pan or wok. Add the chicken and cook until browned, about 10 minutes. Remove with a slotted spoon and place in an ovenproof casserole dish. Heat the oven to 180°C/350°F/Gas mark 4. Add the shallots, mushrooms, turnips, celery and carrots to the pan and cook for 5 minutes, stirring. Add the flour and cook for 1 more minute.

Gradually add the stock, soy sauce and wine, then bring to the boil, stirring. Add the cashew nuts and tomato purée and season well. Pour over the chicken in the casserole dish. Cover and cook in the oven for 45 minutes.

Place the dumpling ingredients in a bowl. Stir in 125 ml/4 fl oz of cold water and knead together to form a dough. Divide into eight pieces and roll these into balls. Uncover the casserole and place the dumplings on top of the chicken mixture. Return to the oven, uncovered, until cooked through, about 15 minutes. Serve.

Chicken Curry with Coconut and Lime

All the different flavours in this exotic-tasting curry marry wonderfully to produce a slightly sweet sauce with a sharp kick provided by the chilli. If you think it is too hot, simply reduce the quantity of chilli added.

serves 4

I Tbsp vegetable oil	350 g/12 oz chicken
2 garlic cloves, crushed	breast, boned and
I red onion, halved and	skinned
sliced	300 ml/½ pt chicken stock
½ tsp garam masala	300 ml/½ pt coconut milk
½ tsp ground cumin	2 Tbsp light soy sauce
½ tsp ground coriander	Juice and grated zest of
½ tsp dried lemon grass	I lime
½ tsp mild curry	2 Tbsp grated coconut
powder	2 Tbsp chopped fresh
¼ tsp turmeric	coriander
I red chilli, chopped	Cooked rice, to serve

Heat the oil in a large wok or frying pan, then cook the garlic and onion for 5 minutes. Stir in the spices and chilli and cook for 2 minutes. Slice the chicken breast and add, stir-frying for another 5 minutes.

Stir in the stock, coconut milk, soy sauce and lime juice. Bring to the boil, reduce the heat, and simmer until the chicken is cooked through, about 20 minutes. Sprinkle with grated coconut, lime zest and coriander and serve with rice.

Orange Turkey
pan-fry

This orange sauce has an almost caramelized flavour as the maple syrup and
brown sugar bubble away to perfection, blending with the orange
juice and spices to create a sweet, unique flavour.

serves 4	
1 Tbsp vegetable oil	2 Tbsp light soy sauce
4 turkey escalopes, skinned	150 ml/¼ pt chicken stock
2 garlic cloves, crushed	2 Tbsp soft brown sugar
½ tsp ground cumin	2 Tbsp maple syrup
½ tsp ground coriander	1 orange, peeled and segmented
1 leek, sliced	1 Tbsp cornflour
1 green pepper, cut into strips	Parsley sprigs, to garnish
150 ml/¼ pt orange juice	

Heat the oil in a wok or frying pan and stir-fry the turkey for 10 minutes,
turning until browned.

Add the garlic, spices, leek and pepper and stir-fry for 3 to 4 minutes. Add
the orange juice, soy sauce and chicken stock and bring to the boil. Stir in
the brown sugar and maple syrup, reduce the heat and simmer for about
20 minutes.

Add the orange segments to the mixture. Blend the cornflour with 2
tablespoons of cold water to form a smooth paste. Add to the sauce and
bring to the boil, stirring until thickened and clear. Cook for 1 minute and
serve garnished with parsley.

Chicken, Apricot and Coriander Casserole

This recipe uses apricots and herbs to give a slightly Middle Eastern flavour.

serves 4

2 Tbsp vegetable oil	I Tbsp light soy sauce
4 chicken quarters	16 dried apricots
12 baby onions	175 g/6 oz asparagus spears
I tsp ground cinnamon	2 Tbsp cornflour
I tsp ground coriander	2 Tbsp chopped, fresh
2.5 cm/I in piece fresh	coriander
root ginger, grated	Salt and ground black
600 ml/I pt chicken stock	pepper

Heat the oil in a large wok or frying pan and cook the chicken for 15 minutes, turning until browned. Remove the chicken with a draining spoon, and then place in a large, ovenproof casserole dish. Heat the oven to 180°C/350°F/Gas mark 4. Add the onions, cinnamon, coriander and ginger to the pan and cook for 5 minutes. Transfer to the casserole dish and stir in the stock, soy sauce and dried apricots. Cover and cook for about 45 minutes.

Remove the casserole from the oven and stir in the trimmed asparagus. Return to the oven until the chicken has cooked through, about 30 minutes. Blend the cornflour with 2 tablespoons of cold water. Remove the casserole from the oven and stir in the cornflour and coriander. Reheat to thicken, season well and serve.

Lemon Chicken

This recipe has a piquant sauce which really gets the taste buds going.

serves 4

8 boned chicken thighs	150 ml/¼ pt chicken
I Tbsp vegetable oil	stock
2 Tbsp butter	Juice and grated zest of
I onion, cut into 16	I lemon
pieces	I Tbsp light soy sauce
I green pepper, cut	I Tbsp soft brown
into strips	sugar
2.5 cm/I in piece fresh	50 g/2 oz asparagus
root ginger, grated	spears, trimmed

Skin the chicken thighs. Heat the oil and butter in a wok and fry the chicken for 10 minutes. Add the onion, pepper and ginger and cook for 5 minutes, stirring. Add the stock, lemon juice, soy sauce and sugar. Bring to the boil, reduce the heat, and simmer for 15 minutes. Add the asparagus and cook for a further 10 minutes. Sprinkle with the lemon zest and serve.

Chicken Filo Pie

Filo pastry is easy and convenient to use for both sweet and savoury dishes.

serves 6

for the filling		
2 Tbsp butter	150 ml/¼ pt milk	8 sheets of filo pastry,
I leek, sliced	2 Tbsp light soy sauce	thawed
350 g/12 oz chicken	50 g/2 oz sundried	2 Tbsp butter, melted
breast meat,	tomatoes in oil,	
chopped	drained and sliced	
25 g/I oz plain flour	I celery stick, sliced	
25 g/I oz blanched	50 g/2 oz baby corn	
almonds, chopped	cobs, sliced	
150 ml/¼ pt chicken	2 Tbsp chopped fresh	
stock	rosemary	
	Ground black pepper	

Melt the butter for the filling in a saucepan, and sauté the leek and chicken for 5 minutes. Add the flour and cook for I minute. Stir in the almonds, chicken stock, milk, and soy sauce and bring to the boil. Add the tomatoes, celery, corn and rosemary. Season well.

Heat the oven to 200°C/400°F/Gas mark 6. Place the chicken mixture in a deep pie dish. Lay a sheet of filo pastry on top of the dish and brush with melted butter. Repeat once more. Cut the remaining pastry into triangles and lay on top in layers, brushing with melted butter. Cook in the oven until golden, about 20 to 25 minutes. Serve.

Stir-fried Duck

A simple dish, making good use of a less-frequently-used bird. Duck is perfect when cooked with redcurrant jelly and raisins in this risotto-style recipe.

serves 4	
300 g/10 oz duck breast, skinned	2 Tbsp dark soy sauce
2 Tbsp vegetable oil	100 g/4 oz open cap mushrooms, peeled and sliced
1 red onion, sliced	
2 garlic cloves, crushed	150 g/6 oz arborio (risotto) rice
1 tsp Chinese five spice powder	
1 leek, sliced	900 ml/1½ pt chicken stock
50 g/2 oz raisins	
1 red pepper, cut into thin strips	Salt and ground black pepper
2 Tbsp redcurrant jelly	2 Tbsp chopped fresh parsley, to garnish

Cut the duck into thin strips. Heat the oil in a wok and stir-fry the duck, onion, garlic, Chinese five spice powder and leek for 5 minutes. Add the raisins, pepper, redcurrant jelly, soy sauce, mushrooms and rice, and cook for 2 minutes, stirring.

Pour in the stock, then season and cook until all the liquid has been absorbed and the rice is fluffy, about 30 minutes. Sprinkle with fresh parsley and serve.

Duck with Bacon and Redcurrants

Smoked bacon adds a lot of flavour to recipes. It is fairly strong and only needs to be used in small quantities. In this dish it blends perfectly with the duck and redcurrants.

serves 4

175 g/6 oz smoked bacon, chopped	4 Tbsp redcurrant jelly	Fresh celery leaves and redcurrants to
1 Tbsp vegetable oil	1½ Tbsp light soy sauce	garnish (optional)
4 half duck breasts	3 celery sticks, sliced	
450 ml/¾ pt chicken stock	4 tsp cornflour	
	Salt and ground black pepper	

Heat the oven to 180°C/350°F/Gas mark 4. Place the bacon in a shallow flameproof casserole dish and cook over a moderate heat for 2 to 3 minutes. Add the oil and duck breasts and cook for a further 5 minutes, turning until browned.

Stir in the stock, redcurrant jelly, soy sauce and celery. Season and bring to the boil. Cover and cook in the oven until the duck is cooked through, about 30 minutes.

Blend the cornflour with 8 teaspoons of cold water and stir into the dish. Boil until thickened and clear. Season and serve garnished with celery and redcurrants.

Crab Cakes

Serrano peppers are small, very hot peppers. Substitute one jalapeño pepper if necessary. The chillies make these crab cakes quite hot and spicy; so add more or less, depending on your own heat tolerance.

makes 4 crab cakes	
Two 175 g/6 oz cans white crab meat, with juices from can	1 Tbsp Dijon mustard
	1 Tbsp mayonnaise
2 fresh serrano chillies, seeded and chopped	1½ tsp light soy sauce
	¼ tsp pepper
1½ Tbsp finely chopped fresh coriander	1 tsp butter
	1 tsp vegetable oil
50 g/2 oz breadcrumbs	Salsa, tartar or cocktail sauce, to serve
1 Tbsp finely chopped onion	

Empty the crab meat with juice into a large bowl. Using a fork, mix in the remaining ingredients, stirring thoroughly. Store in the refrigerator for a few hours or overnight, to allow the flavours to blend.

To cook, form into patties – four large or six small. Cook lightly in the butter and oil, for about 5 to 7 minutes per side. Serve with salsa, tartar or cocktail sauce and lemon wedges if desired.

Scallops with Pecan Crust

This recipe makes a very rich meal. It is best served with a light tossed salad, white wine and fruit.

serves 4

1 kg/2 lb large bay scallops (or sea scallops cut in half)
150 g/5 oz ground pecans
150 g/5 oz fresh breadcrumbs
2 eggs
50 g/2 oz plain flour
2 Tbsp unsalted butter
3 Tbsp oil

for the sauce
2 Tbsp unsalted butter
2 Tbsp plain flour
375 ml/12 fl oz white wine
1 Tbsp light soy sauce

If the scallops are large, cut them in half. Rinse them with cold water and then pat them dry with kitchen paper. The drier they are, the better the coating will stick. Place the ground pecans into a bowl with the breadcrumbs and stir. In a separate bowl, lightly beat the eggs. Put the flour in a third bowl. To coat the scallops, first roll each one in the flour, then dip in the egg and finally roll in the pecan mixture. Make sure each scallop is thoroughly coated.

Melt the butter and oil in a pan, and fry the scallops until golden, about 10 minutes. Using a slotted spoon, remove them to a bowl and keep warm in the oven at 130°C/250°F/Gas mark ½ while you make the sauce. Save the pan drippings for the sauce.

For the sauce, add the 2 tablespoons of butter to the pan drippings and stir until melted. Add the flour, stirring constantly, until a smooth paste is formed. Slowly stir in the wine, a little at a time, mixing well. Add the soy sauce. Simmer for about 5 minutes. It should be thick enough to coat a spoon, but not too thick. Spoon the sauce over the scallops and serve.

Fish Bites

A really "meaty" white fish is best for cubing in this recipe.

serves 4

300 g/10 oz white fish, cubed
2 Tbsp light soy sauce
1 Tbsp lemon juice
2 Tbsp dry white wine
½ tsp ground ginger
1 large courgette
1 large carrot

1 Tbsp chopped, fresh dill to garnish

for the sauce
150 ml/12 fl oz dry white wine
5 Tbsp fish stock
1 Tbsp light soy sauce

2 Tbsp ginger wine
1 tsp fresh root ginger, grated
1 Tbsp cornflour
2 spring onions, chopped

Place the fish in a shallow dish. Mix the soy sauce, lemon juice, white wine and ginger. Pour over the fish, cover and marinate for 2 hours.

Meanwhile, using a vegetable peeler, slice the courgette and carrot lengthwise into thin strips. Blanch the vegetables in boiling water for 1 minute, and then plunge them into cold water. Leave until cold. Soak four wooden skewers in cold water for 30 minutes.

Remove the fish from the marinade, reserving the liquid together with the vegetable strips. Pat the vegetables dry with kitchen paper. Wrap a piece of courgette around each fish cube and then a piece of carrot. Thread four cubes onto each wooden skewer and brush them with the marinade. Grill for 10 minutes, turning once and brushing with the marinade.

To make the sauce, heat the wine, stock, soy sauce, ginger wine and ginger in a pan. Bring to the boil. Blend the cornflour with 2 tablespoons of cold water and then add to the pan. Return to the boil until thickened, add the spring onions and cook for 1 minute. Sprinkle with dill and then serve.

Barbecued Fish Steaks

Thick fish steaks or fillets, such as cod, salmon or tuna, are ideal for this recipe.

serves 4

Four 175 g/6 oz fish steaks, such as cod, sea bass, salmon or swordfish
150 ml/¼ pt sunflower oil
150 ml/¼ pt red wine vinegar
1 Tbsp soft brown sugar
2 Tbsp light soy sauce
60 ml/2 fl oz dry white wine
1 garlic clove, crushed
1 tsp fennel seeds
1 head fennel, trimmed and cut into 8 pieces
2 celery sticks, cut into strips
1 red onion, cut into 8 pieces
Grated zest of 1 lime

Place the fish in a shallow dish. Mix the oil, vinegar, sugar, soy sauce, wine, garlic and fennel seeds together. Pour over the fish, cover and marinate for 3 hours.

Remove the fish from the marinade, and place a piece of fish in the centre of four squares of foil or wax paper. Divide the vegetables and lime zest between the fish and wrap the foil or paper around to form a parcel. Spoon 2 tablespoons of the marinade over each and seal completely. Cook on hot barbecue coals or grill until cooked through, about 10 to 15 minutes. Serve hot with salad.

Chilli Cod and Avocado Salsa

This is a dish with a real Mexican theme, and is fairly hot and spicy.

serves 4

for the avocado salsa	4 cod fillets, skinned
I large ripe avocado	I Tbsp lime juice
2 Tbsp lemon juice	I onion, chopped
I tomato, seeded and chopped	I red pepper, chopped
I onion, finely chopped	2 garlic cloves, crushed
Ground black pepper	2 red chillies, chopped
	2 Tbsp light soy sauce
	150 ml/¼ pt fish stock
	I tsp chilli powder

To make up the avocado salsa, first halve and seed the avocado, peel and place in a blender or food processor. Add the lemon juice and blend for 10 seconds until smooth. Transfer to a bowl, adding the tomato and onion. Season well. Cover and chill until required.

Place the cod fillets on 4 large squares of foil. Put the lime juice, onion, red pepper, garlic, chillies, soy sauce, fish stock and chilli powder in a blender and blend for 10 seconds. Spread onto the cod, then wrap the foil around the fish to seal completely. Grill for 10 to 15 minutes and serve with the avocado salsa.

Rice-stuffed Squid

Squid complement this rice-and-olive stuffing which has a distinctly Greek flavour.

serves 4

450 g/I lb baby squid, prepared and cleaned	25 g/I oz chestnut mushrooms, diced
40 g/I ½ oz wild and white rice, mixed	I Tbsp black, pitted olives, chopped
300 ml/½ pt fish stock	I ½ Tbsp capers, chopped
2 Tbsp light soy sauce	I garlic clove, crushed
I small carrot, diced	Olive oil for brushing
I Tbsp baby corn	

Chop the squid tentacles and place in a pan. Add the rices, fish stock, soy sauce, carrot, corn and mushrooms. Cook until the rice is fluffy and the liquid absorbed, about 20 minutes. Add the olives, capers and garlic to the rice. Use the rice mixture to stuff the squid, securing the open end with a toothpick. Brush the squid with oil and grill for 5 to 6 minutes, turning until cooked. Serve.

Sweet and Sour Fish

You can't beat a home-made sweet and sour sauce, especially when it coats
chunks of tender, fried fish. The cornflour helps to keep the fish
in one piece and gives it a delicious, crispy coating.

serves 4

450 g/1 lb cod fillet or haddock	2 garlic cloves, crushed
1 tsp rice wine or sherry	**for the sauce**
1 tsp light soy sauce	4 Tbsp soft brown sugar
1 egg, beaten	2 Tbsp vegetable oil
100 g/4 oz cornflour	6 Tbsp garlic wine vinegar
Oil for frying	2 Tbsp dark soy sauce
100 g/4 oz canned bamboo shoots, drained and chopped	2 tsp cornflour
1 red pepper, cut into thin strips	½ tsp paprika
	1 tsp sesame oil

Skin the fish and cut the flesh into 2.5 cm/1 in cubes. Mix together the rice
wine or sherry, soy sauce and egg. Stir in the fish. Remove the fish cubes
and roll each in the cornflour to coat.

Heat the oil in a wok until almost smoking and add the coated fish. Cook
until crisp and cooked through, about 5 minutes. Remove from the oil with
a slotted spoon, draining on kitchen paper to remove excess oil. Discard
the hot oil, leaving approximately 2 tablespoons in the wok. Add the
vegetables and garlic and stir-fry for 4 minutes. Add the fish and mix well.

Place the sauce ingredients in a pan and stir. Heat gently and pour over the
fish. Pour on the sesame oil and serve.

Mixed Fish Casserole

Delicious saffron scones complement a fish dish perfectly. If you do not have saffron, use a pinch of turmeric in its place.

serves 4	
225 g/8 oz cod fillet	1 green pepper, diced
225 g/8 oz smoked	Salt and ground black
haddock fillet	pepper
225 g/8 oz trout fillet	
2 Tbsp butter	for the scones
25 g/1 oz plain flour	A few strands of saffron
125 ml/4 fl oz dry white	or pinch of turmeric
wine	1 Tbsp boiling water
300 ml/½ pt milk	225 g/8 oz self-raising
2 Tbsp light soy sauce	flour
1 Tbsp creamed	50 g/2 oz butter
horseradish	50 g/2 oz Cheddar
50 g/2 oz button	cheese, grated
mushrooms, sliced	150 ml/¼ pt milk

Skin and de-bone the fish, cutting the flesh into cubes. Melt the butter in a saucepan, add the flour, and cook for 1 minute. Remove from the heat, and add the wine and milk, stirring well. Return to the heat and stir in the soy sauce, horseradish, fish, mushrooms and pepper. Season well and bring to the boil, stirring. Transfer the mixture to a shallow ovenproof dish.

To make the scones, first place the saffron in the boiling water, and infuse for 10 minutes. Heat the oven to 180°C/350°F/Gas mark 4. Sieve the flour into a bowl and rub in the butter to resemble breadcrumbs. Stir in the cheese, saffron threads, liquid and milk. Mix together to form a soft dough. Roll out on a lightly floured surface and cut into eight rounds. Arrange on top of the fish. Bake in the oven until golden, about 45 minutes.

F i l o F i s h P a r c e l s

These parcels are bursting with shellfish and seafood in a creamy chive sauce.

serves 4

for the filling	thawed if frozen, or
2 Tbsp butter	225 g/8 oz fresh
50 g/2 oz plain flour	mussels, clams,
150 ml/¼ pt fish stock	prawns and squid,
150 ml/¼ pt double	shelled and deveined
cream	2 Tbsp chopped fresh
1 Tbsp light soy sauce	chives
2 tsp lemon juice	Salt and ground black
Few drops of Tabasco	pepper
sauce	16 sheets filo pastry
450 g/1 lb seafood,	3 Tbsp butter, melted

Melt the butter for the filling in a pan, add the flour, and cook for 1 minute. Remove from the heat and stir in the fish stock, cream, soy sauce, lemon juice, Tabasco sauce to taste and seafood. Bring to the boil and cook for 5 minutes. Stir in the chives and season well. Let cool slightly.

Heat the oven to 220°C/425°F/Gas mark 7. Lay four sheets of filo pastry on a work surface. Brush with melted butter and place another sheet on top of each. Repeat twice more. Spoon one quarter of the fish mixture into the centre of each pastry sheet. Brush the edges with butter and bring the edges up to enclose the filling. Pull together at the top to close. Brush the parcels with butter and place on a baking sheet. Bake in the oven until golden, about 10 minutes. Serve warm.

G r i l l e d S a l m o n w i t h R o s e m a r y

Fresh rosemary gives a wonderful aroma and flavour to this dish.

serves 4

Four 100 g/4 oz salmon	4 garlic cloves, crushed
steaks or 450 g/1 lb	2 Tbsp light soy sauce
salmon tail piece,	3 rosemary sprigs
filleted and skinned	6 Tbsp olive oil
	1 Tbsp lime juice
for the marinade	Salt and ground black
1 Tbsp cider vinegar	pepper

Lay the salmon in an ovenproof dish. Mix the liquid marinade ingredients together and pour over the fish. Cover and marinate for 2 hours. Remove the salmon from the marinade and sprinkle with rosemary. Cook under the grill, turning once or until cooked through, about 10 to 15 minutes. Serve.

Fish Kebabs

Ideal for a summer party, these kebabs make a delicious starter
or a good alternative to meat.

serves 4	
for the marinade	150 ml/¼ pt fish stock
3 Tbsp light soy sauce	625 g/1½ lb cod fillets
2 garlic cloves, crushed	4 small baking
Few drops of Tabasco	potatoes, quartered
sauce	2 red peppers, sliced
2 Tbsp olive oil	into large squares
1 Tbsp cider vinegar	12 large mushrooms
2 tsp black treacle	3 Tbsp olive oil
1 red chilli, sliced	Vegetable oil

For the marinade, mix together the soy sauce, garlic, Tabasco sauce, olive
oil, cider vinegar, black treacle, red chilli and fish stock. Cut the fish into
3 to 5 cm/1½ to 2 in cubes. Pour the marinade over the fish and marinate
in the refrigerator for several hours or overnight. Pre-cook the potatoes
to shorten the barbecuing time. Either use a microwave for 4 minutes
on high or boil them, quartered but with skins, until just tender, about
15 minutes.

To make the kebabs, use either metal or wooden skewers which have
been soaked in water for 30 minutes. Then thread the fish cubes,
potatoes, peppers and mushrooms onto the skewers, alternating the
ingredients. Brush the vegetables with olive oil.

Brush the grill with vegetable oil to prevent sticking. Barbecue the kebabs
over hot coals, approximately 5 minutes per side.

rice, pasta and noodles

Spicy Green Rice

There is something very pleasing both to the eye and the palate about a mixture of green vegetables. Perfectly offset by the wild and brown rice, this really is a feast for the eyes.

serves 4

2 Tbsp olive oil	½ tsp ground cinnamon
50 g/2 oz okra	50 g/2 oz chopped
I courgette, cut into	almonds
thin strips	75 g/3 oz wild rice
2 celery sticks, sliced	75 g/3 oz brown rice
2½ oz green beans,	2 Tbsp light soy sauce
trimmed	600 ml/I pt vegetable
I green pepper, cut	stock
into strips	5 Tbsp double cream
I green chilli, sliced	2 Tbsp chopped fresh
I tsp chilli powder	parsley
I tsp ground coriander	Ground black pepper
I tsp garam masala	

Heat the olive oil in a wok or frying pan and fry the vegetables for 5 minutes. Add the spices, almonds and rices and cook for I minute. Stir in the soy sauce and stock and bring to the boil. Reduce the heat, simmering until all the liquid has been absorbed and the rice is fully cooked, about 30 minutes.

Stir in the cream and half of the parsley and add seasoning. Transfer to a warmed serving dish, sprinkle with remaining parsley and serve.

Bean and Pasta Soup

Pasta is ideal as a filler in soups, making them really chunky and wholesome.

serves 4

100 g/4 oz mixed, dried
beans, soaked
overnight
1.75 l/3 pt vegetable stock
2 Tbsp olive oil
1 leek, sliced
2 garlic cloves, crushed
200 g/7 oz can chopped
tomatoes

3 Tbsp light soy sauce
100 g/4 oz small pasta
shapes
Ground black pepper
25 g/1 oz Parmesan
cheese, freshly grated
1 Tbsp chopped fresh
basil

Drain the soaked beans and rinse them under cold running water. Place in a large saucepan and add the stock. Bring to the boil, then boil vigorously for 10 minutes. Reduce the heat to a simmer and cook for 1½ hours. Remove half of the beans with a draining spoon, place them in a blender or food processor and process for 20 seconds. Return to the pan.

In a separate pan, heat the oil and cook the leek and garlic for 5 minutes. Add the canned tomatoes and soy sauce and cook for 2 to 3 minutes. Add the tomato mixture to the pan of beans, with the puréed beans. Stir in the pasta and bring to the boil. Cook until the pasta is done, about 10 minutes. Season with pepper and ladle into a warmed soup tureen. Sprinkle with Parmesan and basil and serve.

Hot and Sour Beef Noodles

Rice noodles are thinner than egg noodles and have a translucent appearance.

serves 4

350 g/12 oz rice
noodles
1 Tbsp sesame oil

for the sauce
1 Tbsp groundnut oil
225 g/8 oz braising
steak, cut into strips

1 red pepper, sliced
2 Tbsp dark soy sauce
1 Tbsp chilli oil
1 Tbsp Chinese rice
vinegar
4 spring onions, sliced
1 tsp soft brown sugar

Soak the rice noodles in warm water for 25 minutes. Drain and toss in the sesame oil. Meanwhile, heat the groundnut oil in a wok, and stir-fry the beef and red pepper for 7 minutes. Add the soy sauce, chilli oil, vinegar, spring onions and sugar. Simmer for 5 minutes. Place the noodles in a warmed serving dish and spoon on the beef mixture. Serve immediately.

Hot Pasta Salad

Pasta salads are usually cold but this colourful recipe really benefits from being eaten warm, as it brings out the flavours in the dressing.

serves 4

for the dressing

2 Tbsp light soy sauce
60 ml/2 fl oz dry white wine
1 Tbsp olive oil
1 Tbsp sesame oil
2 Tbsp balsamic vinegar
2 Tbsp chopped fresh thyme or parsley
2 tsp wholegrain mustard
225 g/8 oz wholewheat pasta shapes

1 tsp salt
1 Tbsp vegetable oil
1 red pepper, sliced
1 green pepper, sliced
1 yellow pepper, sliced
50 g/2 oz mangetout
100 g/4 oz small cauliflower flowerets
1 carrot, cut into strips
50 g/2 oz sundried tomatoes in oil, drained and sliced
1 Tbsp sesame seeds, to garnish
Ground black pepper

Cook the pasta in boiling salted water until *al dente* ("with bite" or still firm), 8 to 10 minutes. Meanwhile, heat the oil in a large wok or frying pan and stir-fry the peppers, mangetout, cauliflower, carrot and tomatoes for 7 minutes. Place the dressing ingredients in a pan and simmer for 2 to 3 minutes.

Drain the pasta and place in a warmed serving dish. Top with the vegetable mixture and pour on the dressing. Sprinkle with sesame seeds, season with pepper and toss well. Serve immediately.

Chilli Chicken
Noodles

This recipe has a wonderful bright-red sauce coating the noodles, making a fiery looking dish that tastes as hot as it looks!

serves 4

225 g/8 oz thin, dried-egg noodles	2 Tbsp light soy sauce
225 g/8 oz boneless chicken breast	1 tsp chilli oil
Oil for deep frying	2 Tbsp tomato purée
1 Tbsp groundnut oil	2 tsp soft brown sugar
1 tsp Chinese five spice powder	4 spring onions, sliced
1 tsp chilli powder	50 g/2 oz canned bamboo shoots, drained
2 garlic cloves, crushed	1 red chilli, chopped

Cook the noodles in boiling water for 5 minutes. Drain and place in a bowl of cold water until required. Slice the chicken breast. Heat the oil for deep frying in a wok until almost smoking. Fry the chicken strips for 3 to 4 minutes. Remove with a draining spoon and drain on kitchen paper.

Heat the groundnut oil in a wok and cook the spices, garlic and soy sauce for 30 seconds. Drain the noodles and add to the wok with the chilli oil, tomato purée, sugar, spring onions, bamboo shoots and chilli. Stir in the chicken and and cook for 4 to 5 minutes. Serve.

Mushroom Pasta

Different varieties of mushrooms add extra interest to this wonderful pasta
sauce. Any tagliatelle may be used in the recipe; try using spinach,
tomato, or garlic flavour pastas for a change.

serves 4

225 g/8 oz dried or fresh tagliatelle	100 g/4 oz wild mushrooms
1 tsp salt	100 g/4 oz oyster mushrooms
for the sauce	2 Tbsp dark soy sauce
50 g/2 oz butter	150 ml/¼ pt vegetable stock
2 garlic cloves, crushed	2 Tbsp chopped fresh parsley
1 red onion, quartered	Ground black pepper
100 g/4 oz shiitake mushrooms	

Cook the pasta in boiling salted water for 8 to 10 minutes if dried and for
5 minutes if fresh until *al dente*.

Meanwhile, melt the butter in a saucepan, and fry the garlic and onion for
5 minutes. Add the mushrooms, soy sauce and stock and cook for 4 to 5
minutes.

Drain the pasta and return to the pan. Stir in the mushroom mixture,
tossing the pasta to mix thoroughly. Sprinkle with parsley and season well.
Spoon into a warmed serving dish and serve immediately.

Noodles with Peanut Sauce

Noodles tossed in a spicy peanut sauce make a quick vegetarian satay dish.

serves 4		
225 g/8 oz broccoli flowerets	2 Tbsp groundnut oil	I Tbsp chilli sauce
I carrot, cut into strips	150 ml/¼ pt crunchy peanut butter	450 g/I lb egg noodles
I leek, sliced	225 ml/7 fl oz coconut milk	
I courgette, sliced	I Tbsp lime juice	
4 spring onions, sliced	2 Tbsp light soy sauce	
I green chilli, sliced		

Cook all the prepared vegetables in the groundnut oil in a wok or large frying pan for 3 to 4 minutes. Meanwhile, place the peanut butter, coconut milk, lime juice, soy sauce and chilli sauce in a pan. Stir over a low heat until well mixed and hot.

Cook the noodles in boiling water for 2 to 3 minutes. Drain and add to the vegetables. Pour on the peanut sauce and serve immediately.

Pasta and Spinach Soufflé

The three colours of the pasta stand out from the golden colour of the soufflé.

serves 4	
100 g/4 oz tricolour pasta shapes	3 Tbsp light soy sauce
½ tsp salt	Ground black pepper
450 g/I lb fresh spinach	Pinch of ground nutmeg
50 g/2 oz butter	3 eggs, separated
3 Tbsp plain flour	100 g/4 oz Emmenthal cheese, grated
225 ml/7 fl oz milk	I egg white

Grease a 1.25 1/2 pt soufflé dish. Cook the pasta in boiling salted water, 8 to 10 minutes. Drain and reserve. Blanch the spinach, 2 minutes (with stems removed) in boiling water. Drain in a sieve, pressing down to remove the moisture. Heat the oven to 190°C/375°F/Gas mark 5. Melt the butter in a saucepan, stir in the flour and cook I minute. Remove from the heat, stir in the milk and soy sauce. Return to the heat and bring to the boil, stirring until thickened. Season with pepper and nutmeg and cool.

Beat the egg yolks, one at a time, into the sauce and add 75 g/3 oz of the cheese. Stir in the drained pasta and spinach. Whisk the egg whites until peaks form and then fold into the mixture. Spoon into the soufflé dish and sprinkle with the remaining cheese. Stand the dish on a baking sheet. Cook in the oven until risen and set, about 30 minutes. Serve immediately.

Scrambled Pasta

A complete meal in a pan, this is a perfect brunch or suppertime dish.

serves 4

100 g/4 oz small, dried pasta shapes
½ tsp salt
1 Tbsp vegetable oil
4 large flavoured sausages, such as leek, pepper, herb or mustard
6 slices smoked bacon, trimmed and chopped

2 tomatoes, seeded and chopped
6 eggs, beaten
5 Tbsp milk
1 Tbsp light soy sauce
1 Tbsp butter
50 g/2 oz Cheddar cheese, grated
2 Tbsp double cream
Ground black pepper

Cook the pasta in boiling salted water until *al dente*, about 10 minutes. Drain well.

Meanwhile, heat the oil in a large wok or frying pan and cook the sausages for 10 minutes. Remove from the pan, slice and return to the pan with the chopped bacon and tomatoes. Cook for 5 minutes, stirring. Stir in the drained pasta.

Beat together the eggs, milk and soy sauce. Add the butter to the pan and pour in the egg mixture. Cook, stirring, for 3 to 4 minutes. Stir in half of the cheese and cook for a further 2 minutes. Stir in the cream and then spoon the mixture into a warmed serving dish. Sprinkle with remaining cheese, season and serve.

Salmon and Haddock Rice

There are three varieties of rice in this simple recipe, all adding to the dish in their own way. The wild rice adds colour, the brown rice a nutty flavour, and the arborio or risotto rice a great texture.

serves 4

2 Tbsp vegetable oil
I leek, sliced
I garlic clove, crushed
I tsp dried lemon grass
I tsp curry powder
¼ tsp turmeric
50 g/2 oz wild rice
50 g/2 oz arborio (risotto) rice
50 g/2 oz brown rice
225 g/8 oz salmon fillet, skinned and cubed

225 g/8 oz smoked haddock fillet, skinned and cubed
450 ml/¾ pt fish stock
150 ml/¼ pt vermouth
2 Tbsp light soy sauce
Salt and ground black pepper
2 Tbsp chopped fresh dill

Heat the oil in a large wok or frying pan and cook the leek and garlic for 3 minutes. Add the lemon grass, curry powder and turmeric and cook for a further 2 minutes. Add the three rices and cook for I minute, stirring.

Add the salmon and smoked haddock, and then pour in the fish stock, vermouth and soy sauce. Season and bring to the boil. Reduce the heat to a simmer and cook until the rice is cooked through and the liquid has been absorbed, about 30 minutes. Sprinkle with chopped dill and serve.

Pasta Gratin

Brightly coloured peppers always look spectacular, especially when combined
with sundried tomatoes, garlic and olive oil for a true Mediterranean flavour.

serves 4

350 g/12 oz dried pasta
bows
1 tsp salt
1 Tbsp olive oil
2 garlic cloves, crushed
1 red pepper, cut into
thin strips
1 green pepper, cut
into thin strips

75 g/3 oz sundried
tomatoes in oil,
drained and cut
into strips
2 Tbsp light soy sauce
150 ml/¼ pt double
cream
1 Tbsp lemon juice
2 Tbsp chopped fresh
thyme or parsley

1 egg, beaten
Ground black pepper
75 g/3 oz Mozzarella
cheese, grated

Cook the pasta in boiling salted water until *al dente*, 8 to 10 minutes.
Drain well.

Meanwhile, heat the oil in a wok or frying pan and fry the garlic, peppers
and tomatoes for 5 minutes. Mix the soy sauce, cream, lemon juice, thyme
or parsley and egg. Season. Place the pasta and pepper mixture in a
shallow heatproof dish. Pour on the cream mixture.

Sprinkle the dish with the Mozzarella cheese. Cook under the grill until
browned, about 5 minutes. Serve.

Lamb Cutlets with Tomato Relish

A simple fresh tomato and herb relish, spiced up with horseradish, is perfect with tender juicy lamb cutlets.

serves 4

8 lamb rib cutlets
2 Tbsp dark soy sauce
1 Tbsp olive oil
1 garlic clove, crushed
2 Tbsp garlic wine vinegar
2 rosemary sprigs

for the relish
4 tomatoes, seeded and chopped

1 Tbsp soft brown sugar
4 tsp red wine vinegar
2 spring onions, sliced
1 Tbsp horseradish sauce
1 Tbsp dark soy sauce
1 Tbsp chopped fresh rosemary

Trim the excess fat from each lamb cutlet. Scrape the bone with a knife until clean. Place the lamb in a shallow dish. Mix the soy sauce, olive oil, garlic, garlic wine vinegar and rosemary together. Pour over the lamb. Cover and marinate for 2 hours.

Meanwhile, place the relish ingredients in a pan and simmer for 5 minutes. Remove the lamb from the marinade and grill for 15 minutes, turning until cooked. Re-heat the tomato relish until hot, and then serve immediately with the grilled lamb.

Pork in Filo Parcels

This is a variation on Cordon bleu, using ham and cheese as a topping for meat, but the flavour is slightly Italian because of the sundried tomatoes and herbs.

serves 4

4 pork escalopes
2 Tbsp vegetable oil
8 sheets of filo pastry
2 Tbsp butter, melted

for the topping
100 g/4 oz ham, diced
1 Tbsp light soy sauce

50 g/2 oz Mozzarella
    cheese, grated
1 Tbsp chopped fresh
    thyme
25 g/1 oz sundried
    tomatoes in oil,
    drained and chopped
Ground black pepper

Place the pork escalopes between two sheets of greaseproof paper and beat with a meat mallet until 5 mm/¼ in thick. Fry in the vegetable oil in a frying pan or skillet for 10 minutes, turning. Remove from the pan and drain well on kitchen paper to remove excess oil.

Heat the oven to 190°C/375°F/Gas mark 5. Lay four sheets of filo pastry side by side on a work surface. Brush with butter. Place a further sheet on top of each. Mix the topping ingredients together. Place a pork escalope in the centre of each sheet of pastry and top each with a quarter of the ham mixture.

Brush the edges of the pastry with butter and fold around the escalope. Brush with butter and place on a baking sheet. Bake in the oven until the parcels are cooked through, about 20 minutes. Serve.

Pan-fried Beef with Peppercorn Sauce

This classic recipe benefits greatly from the addition of soy sauce. Always remember to ignite and extinguish the brandy before returning the pan to the heat.

serves 4

4 sirloin steaks	I Tbsp vegetable oil
3 Tbsp mixed	2 Tbsp brandy
peppercorns,	I Tbsp light soy sauce
crushed	150 ml/¼ pt double
2 Tbsp butter	cream

Trim the steaks of any excess fat. Press the crushed peppercorns onto each side of the steaks. Heat the butter and oil in a wok or frying pan and cook the steaks for 3 minutes on each side. Remove from the pan and keep warm.

Remove the pan from the heat and add the brandy. Ignite and leave to burn out. Stir in the soy sauce and cream. Return the steaks to the pan and heat for a further 3 to 4 minutes. Serve.

Spicy Roast pork

Tender pork coated in plum glaze and baked with fresh plums looks sensational.
As an alternative to pork tenderloin, use turkey breast.

serves 4

675 g/1½ lb pork tenderloin

2 Tbsp vegetable oil

2 Tbsp dark soy sauce

2 tsp Chinese five spice powder

1 tsp ground cumin

½ tsp chilli powder

125 ml/4 fl oz plum jam, sieved

1 Tbsp honey

100 g/4 oz plums, seeded and quartered

Heat the oven to 180°C/350°F/Gas mark 4. Trim any excess fat from the meat. Heat the oil in a roasting tin over a moderate heat. Add the pork and brown all over. Place the soy sauce, spices, plum jam and honey in a saucepan and heat until liquid. Brush over the pork, reserving any glaze.

Cook the pork in the oven for 30 minutes. Brush with the remaining glaze. Return to the oven until cooked through, about 25 to 30 minutes. Arrange the plum quarters around the pork 10 minutes before the end of cooking time. Slice and serve with the cooking liquor.

Lamb Hot Pot

The soy sauce really makes the juices in this favourite hot pot extra special.

serves 4

675 g/1½ lb boned shoulder of lamb	2 tsp chopped fresh thyme
3 Tbsp vegetable oil	Salt and ground black pepper
450 g/1 lb leek, sliced	
2 carrots, sliced	2 Tbsp dark soy sauce
100 g/4 oz French beans, trimmed	450 ml/¾ pt lamb stock
1 kg/2 lb potatoes, sliced	150 ml/¼ pt dry white wine

Heat the oven to 170°C/325°F/Gas mark 3. Trim the lamb of any excess fat and cut the meat into 2.5 cm/1 in cubes. Heat the oil in a frying pan or wok and fry the lamb, turning until browned. Layer the lamb, leeks, carrots, beans and potatoes in a large ovenproof casserole dish, sprinkling each layer with thyme and seasoning, reserving enough potato to cover the surface. Mix the soy sauce, stock and wine together. Pour over the meat and top with a layer of potatoes.

Cover and cook in the oven for 2 hours. Uncover the casserole and increase the temperature to 220°C/425°F/Gas mark 7. Cook the casserole until the potatoes are golden and crisp, about 30 minutes. Serve.

Fruity Burgers

These burgers are succulent and slightly sweet and have a terrific flavour. Use different dried fruits, such as mango or peach, to vary the flavour.

serves 4

450 g/1 lb minced beef	1 Tbsp chopped fresh coriander
½ onion, chopped	
2 Tbsp dark soy sauce	1 garlic clove, crushed
Salt and ground black pepper	½ tsp ground coriander
75 g/3 oz no-soak dried apricots, finely chopped	2 Tbsp vegetable oil
	Burger buns, salad, onion slices and dill pickles, to serve

Place all the ingredients except the oil in a mixing bowl. Mix together well with your hands, and divide into four equal portions. Shape the meat into four flat rounds on a lightly floured board. Heat the oil in a frying pan or wok and cook the burgers, turning once until cooked through, about 10 minutes. Place each burger in a bun with lettuce, onion and dill pickles, and serve.

Beef Stir-fry

Dried mushrooms are a little bit of a luxury, but well worth purchasing. They add a unique, strong flavour to dishes and need only be used in small quantities.

serves 4

450 g/1 lb lean steak
2 Tbsp vegetable oil
3 Tbsp dark soy sauce
1 red chilli, chopped
1 cm/½ in piece fresh root ginger, grated
2 Tbsp red wine vinegar
2 Tbsp cornflour

for the stir-fry
4 dried Chinese mushrooms
1 Tbsp vegetable oil

4 spring onions, cut lengthways
2 celery sticks, sliced
1 carrot, cut into thin strips
1 courgette, cut into thin strips
100 g/4 oz baby corn cobs, halved lengthways
100 g/4 oz cauliflower flowerets
1 Tbsp chilli sauce

Cut the beef into thin strips, cutting across the grain. Place in a shallow dish. Mix half of the oil, the soy sauce, chilli, ginger and vinegar together and pour over the beef. Cover and marinate for 1 hour.

Remove the beef from the marinade with a draining spoon, reserving the marinade. Roll the beef in the cornflour.

Reconstitute the Chinese mushrooms in boiling water for 20 minutes. Drain well. Heat the remaining oil in a wok and stir-fry the beef for 4 minutes. Add the spring onions, celery, carrot, courgette, corn and cauliflower, and stir-fry for a further 4 minutes. Add the reserved marinade to the wok with the chilli sauce and stir-fry for 1 minute and serve.

Lamb with Cranberry Sauce

Cranberries are traditionally associated with turkey, but are just as good with lamb. Use fresh fruit if possible, or frozen cranberries straight from the freezer. If thawed before use, they will disintegrate during cooking.

serves 4

Eight 75 g/3 oz lamb loin cutlets, boned
2 Tbsp vegetable oil
100 g/4 oz button mushrooms, halved
300 ml/½ pt lamb stock
2 Tbsp dark soy sauce

4 Tbsp cranberry sauce
150 ml/¼ pt cranberry juice
1 tsp tomato purée
25 g/1 oz cranberries
1 Tbsp chopped fresh coriander

1½ Tbsp cornflour
2 Tbsp cold water

Trim the excess fat from the lamb. Heat the oil in a large frying pan or wok and fry the lamb for 5 minutes, turning until browned. Add the mushrooms and cook for a further 2 to 3 minutes. Add the stock, soy sauce, cranberry sauce, cranberry juice and tomato purée. Simmer for 15 minutes, turning the lamb.

Stir in the cranberries and coriander. Blend the cornflour with 2 tablespoons of cold water and stir into the pan. Bring to the boil, stirring until thickened and clear. Serve.

Kidneys in Sherry Sauce

Kidneys can be difficult to prepare, so ask your butcher to core them for you.

serves 4

16 shallots	I bay leaf
3 Tbsp butter	3 Tbsp dry sherry
I Tbsp vegetable oil	2 Tbsp dark soy sauce
225 g/8 oz chestnut	450 ml/¾ pt lamb stock
mushrooms, halved	A few drops of Tabasco
12 lamb kidneys,	sauce
skinned and cored	Salt and ground black
2 celery sticks, sliced	pepper
2 Tbsp plain flour	Cooked rice, to serve

Halve the shallots. Melt the butter and oil in a large frying pan or wok, and cook the shallots and mushrooms for 3 to 4 minutes. Add the kidneys and celery and cook for 5 minutes. Stir in the flour and cook for I more minute. Add the bay leaf, sherry, soy sauce, stock and Tabasco to taste. Cover and simmer until the kidneys are cooked through, about 25 minutes. Serve with freshly cooked rice.

Beef with Pecan Sauce

Serve immediately after the dish is cooked for perfect results.

serves 4

450 g/I lb braising	150 ml/¼ pt red wine
steak, cut into strips	I Tbsp soy sauce
I onion, sliced	4 Tbsp lemon juice
3 Tbsp balsamic	Ground black pepper
vinegar	I tsp ground cinnamon
I Tbsp dark soy sauce	175 g/6 oz pecan
	pieces, crushed
for the sauce	I Tbsp plain flour
6 Tbsp olive oil	6 Tbsp double cream
3 Tbsp butter	2 Tbsp chopped fresh
300 ml/½ pt beef stock	coriander

Place the beef in a shallow dish. Add the onion, vinegar and soy sauce. Cover and marinate for 2 hours. Heat the oil and butter in a casserole dish. Remove the beef from the marinade, reserving the onion. Cook the beef in the butter, turning until browned all over, about 10 minutes.

Add the reserved onion, stock, wine, soy sauce, lemon juice, seasoning and cinnamon. Cover and simmer until the beef is tender, about 1½ hours. Mix the pecans and flour together. Stir into the stock with the cream. Simmer for 5 minutes. Garnish with coriander and serve.

Lamb Couscous

Couscous is a creamy, nutty alternative to rice. Used extensively in African recipes, it is easy to cook and steams over the meat sauce for added flavour.

75 g/3 oz dried chickpeas soaked overnight, or 400 g/ 14 oz can cooked chickpeas, drained
100 g/4 oz butter
450 g/1 lb neck of lamb trimmed of fat, and cubed
1 tsp salt
1 tsp ground black pepper
1 tsp ground ginger
¼ tsp turmeric
¼ tsp ground cinnamon
¼ tsp cayenne pepper
2 red onions, quartered
2 coriander sprigs
1 carrot, cut into chunks
4 baby turnips, quartered
600 ml/1 pt lamb stock
2 Tbsp dark soy sauce
225 g/8 oz couscous
600 ml/1 pt vegetable stock

Drain the chickpeas and place in a large pan. Cover with water and bring to the boil. Boil rapidly for 10 minutes. Drain and rinse.

Melt 6 tablespoons of the butter in a large pan. Add the lamb, salt, pepper, ginger, turmeric, cinnamon, cayenne, onions, coriander, carrot and turnips. Cook for 10 minutes, stirring. Add the stock and soy sauce and stir in the chickpeas. Bring to the boil, cover and simmer for 1½ hours.

Soak the couscous in the vegetable stock until the water has been absorbed, about 30 minutes. Line a colander with a clean, damp tea towel and place the couscous in a mound in the colander. Steam over the lamb for the last 30 minutes of cooking. Stir in 2 tablespoons of melted butter and place on a serving plate. Spoon on the lamb and serve.

chapter

sensational salads

Lamb and Orange Salad

Hot salads are sensational: the mixture of warm and cold ingredients is a treat.
In this recipe, tender chunks of lamb are cooked to perfection in soy sauce
and served with fennel and fresh orange.

serves 4

450 g/1 lb lamb leg steaks	Grated rind of 1 orange
1 Tbsp vegetable oil	for the dressing
1 Tbsp dark soy sauce	3 Tbsp olive oil
1 fennel bulb, sliced	3 Tbsp fresh orange juice
2 oranges, peeled and segmented	$\frac{1}{2}$ tsp prepared horseradish
50 g/2 oz pecan halves	Salt and ground black pepper
100 g/4 oz mixed salad leaves, shredded	2 tsp honey
50 g/2 oz cucumber, sliced and quartered	1 tsp fresh rosemary

Dice the lamb, removing any excess fat. Heat the oil and soy sauce in a
frying pan. Fry the lamb until cooked through, about 10 minutes. Reserve
the lamb and cooking liquor.

Prepare the remaining ingredients and place in a serving bowl. Remove the
lamb from the pan with a slotted spoon and add to the salad.

Mix the dressing ingredients together. Add the cooking liquor from the
pan, stir well and pour over the salad. Serve.

Sweet Potato Salad

The secret to success with this recipe is to cook the sweet potatoes perfectly. If the potatoes are too mushy, the texture of the salad is not as good. When cooked, a fork inserted into the potato should meet some resistance.

serves 6

2 kg/2 lb sweet potatoes
50 g/2 oz celery, thinly sliced
50 g/2 oz green pepper, diced
100 g/4 oz pineapple chunks
50 g/2 oz seedless red grapes
120 ml/4 fl oz mayonnaise
1 tsp mild curry powder
½ tsp ground ginger
1 tsp light soy sauce
2 tsp cider vinegar

Boil the sweet potatoes in water until just tender, about 20 minutes. Cool, peel and cut into 2.5 cm/1 in cubes. Put the potatoes in a bowl with the celery, green pepper, pineapple chunks and grapes.

In a separate bowl, mix the mayonnaise, curry powder, ginger, soy sauce and vinegar. Gently fold the dressing into the sweet potato mixture. Chill before serving.

Winter Fruit Salad

Exotic fresh fruits make this salad unusual and refreshing. The soy dressing complements the fruit perfectly.

serves 4

1 Tbsp light soy sauce
1 Tbsp cider vinegar
Juice of ½ lime
2 tsp soft brown sugar
225 g/8 oz shredded lettuce
300 g/10 oz fresh pineapple, peeled, cored, and cut into bite-sized pieces
1 mango, peeled, pitted, and cut into chunks
1 green dessert apple, cored and cut into bite-sized pieces
75 g/3 oz pitted dates and chopped
2 Tbsp walnut pieces

Mix the soy sauce, vinegar, lime juice and sugar together. Arrange the lettuce in a serving bowl.

Add the pineapple, mango, apple, dates and walnut pieces. Pour the dressing over the top, toss and serve.

Chinese Vegetable and Omelette Salad

Resembling a raw stir-fry, this colourful salad makes use of Chinese vegetables.
Top with sliced omelette for a special finishing touch.

serves 4

450 g/1 lb young cabbage
Oil for deep frying
1 tsp salt
½ tsp ground cinnamon
100 g/4 oz beansprouts
4 spring onions, halved lengthways
50 g/2 oz canned water chestnuts, drained and chopped
1 red pepper, sliced
1 yellow pepper, sliced

50 g/2 oz salted cashew nuts

for the omelette
2 eggs
½ tsp Chinese five spice powder

for the dressing
2 Tbsp light soy sauce
1 Tbsp lime juice
1 Tbsp sesame oil
½ tsp ground ginger

Shred the young cabbage. Heat the oil in a wok and deep fry the cabbage
for 4 to 5 minutes. Drain well on kitchen paper and sprinkle with salt and
cinnamon. Place in a large serving bowl. Top with the beansprouts, spring
onions, water chestnuts, peppers and cashew nuts.

Beat the eggs for the omelette with the Chinese five spice powder. Heat
and oil a 15 cm/6 in omelette pan, then pour in the eggs, tilting the pan to
coat the base with egg. Cook for 2 minutes until the top is set. Flip over
and cook for 2 minutes. Remove and cut into strips. Sprinkle over the
vegetables. Mix the dressing ingredients together, pour on and serve.

Cucumber Salad

Sesame oil has a distinctive taste, so don't substitute any other oil.

serves 4

2 cucumbers (about 675 g/1½ lb), peeled and sliced	1½ tsp light soy sauce
	½ tsp sugar
	½ tsp mild curry powder
2 Tbsp salt	
1 Tbsp sesame oil	1 small garlic clove, crushed
1½ tsp vegetable oil	
4 tsp cider vinegar	

Peel the cucumbers and slice very thinly. Sprinkle with the salt and let sit for 3 hours or longer. Rinse the cucumbers very well, and squeeze them with your hands to remove the liquid. Rinse and squeeze again.

Mix the sesame and vegetable oils, vinegar, soy sauce, sugar, curry powder and crushed garlic. Whisk to blend. Pour over the cucumber, cover and store in the refrigerator for several hours or overnight before serving.

Chinese Chicken Salad

Soy sauce and ginger make a special dressing for this colourful chicken salad.

serves 4

275 g/10 oz cooked chicken, diced	2 heads of chicory
100 g/4 oz canned water chestnuts sliced	for the dressing
	1 Tbsp light soy sauce
50 g/2 oz alfalfa sprouts	1 tsp ground ginger
2 tomatoes, seeded and diced	2 Tbsp walnut oil
	2 Tbsp garlic wine vinegar
4 spring onions, sliced	
1 green pepper, diced	1 Tbsp honey
25 g/1 oz unsalted cashew nuts	1 Tbsp chopped fresh parsley
1 mango, peeled and diced	1 tsp lemon juice

Place the chicken in a bowl with the water chestnuts, alfalfa sprouts, tomatoes, spring onions, pepper, cashew nuts and mango. Mix together gently. Arrange the chicory around a serving plate and spoon the chicken mixture into the centre.

Place all the dressing ingredients in a screwtop jar and shake vigorously to mix. Pour over the salad and serve immediately.

Chinese Coriander Salad

This is a variation on a classic salad, made extra special by the cheese dressing which is poured over the salad ingredients to add flavour superbly.

serves 4

225 g/8 oz head Chinese
leaves or bok choy
1 ripe avocado, seeded
1 yellow pepper, diced
15 g/½ oz coriander,
chopped
6 spring onions, chopped
2 tomatoes, seeded
and diced
4 slices bacon, grilled
and chopped
1 tsp sesame seeds

for the dressing

25 g/1 oz Parmesan
cheese, grated
1 Tbsp sesame oil
4 Tbsp salad oil
1 garlic clove, crushed
1 Tbsp honey
2 Tbsp garlic wine
vinegar
¼ tsp Chinese five spice
powder
2 tsp light soy sauce

Wash the Chinese leaves thoroughly and cut into bite-sized pieces. Chop the avocado, then add to the leaves with the chopped pepper, coriander, spring onions, tomatoes, bacon and sesame seeds.

Mix all the dressing ingredients together and pour over the salad. Toss and serve.

Grated Salad

Celeriac has a strong, fresh aroma and taste and is a delicious addition to this colourful, simple salad. Serve immediately as celeriac discolours quickly.

serves 4	
1 celeriac	for the dressing
2 courgettes	Juice of 1 lime
2 carrots	1 Tbsp light soy sauce
50 g/2 oz desiccated or	1 garlic clove, crushed
fresh coconut, grated	1 Tbsp honey
Ground black pepper	Grated zest of 1 lime,
	to garnish

Trim the celeriac, peel and finely grate. Trim and shred the courgettes and carrots, keeping the vegetables separate.

Arrange the individual vegetables and coconut in small mounds on a large serving platter. Season with pepper.

Mix the dressing ingredients together and pour over the vegetables. Garnish the salad with the grated lime zest and serve immediately.

Carrot, Raisin and Leek Salad

Caraway seeds are used in this semi-sweet salad, as they are ideal for both
sweet and savoury dishes. They have a strong, slightly aniseed flavour.

serves 4

6 large carrots	for the dressing
3 large oranges	**150 ml/¼ pt fresh**
50 g/2 oz raisins	**orange juice**
2 leeks	**2 Tbsp dark soy sauce**
	1 Tbsp maple syrup
	¼ tsp ground nutmeg
	Ground black pepper
	1 tsp caraway seeds

Trim and grate the carrots and place in a bowl. Peel and segment the
oranges and add them to the carrots. Add the raisins. Trim and thinly slice
the leeks, stirring into the carrots.

Mix the dressing ingredients together and pour over the salad. Cover and
chill until required.

Chicory, Bacon and Asparagus Salad

This is a great salad, especially when topped with asparagus and melted cheese.

serves 4

2 heads chicory	for the dressing
4 slices smoked bacon	1 Tbsp light soy sauce
350 g/12 oz asparagus	1 Tbsp lemon juice
spears	2 Tbsp olive oil
25 g/1 oz Emmenthal	1 tsp prepared mustard
cheese, grated	1 Tbsp garlic wine
1 Tbsp pine kernels	vinegar
	Ground black pepper
	2 tsp chopped thyme

Separate the chicory and place them in a shallow ovenproof dish. Grill the bacon for 10 minutes, turning until crisp; chop roughly. Meanwhile, cook the asparagus in boiling water until tender, for 2 to 3 minutes. Drain well and place on top of the chicory. Sprinkle with the bacon, cheese and pine nuts.

Mix the dressing ingredients together and pour over the salad. Cook under the grill until the cheese begins to melt, about 3 to 4 minutes. Serve.

Lentil Salad

Lentils make a nutritious and colourful base for this spicy, warm salad.

serves 4

350 g/12 oz red lentils	100 g/4 oz tomatoes,	2 Tbsp light soy sauce
Dash of salt	seeded and diced	2 Tbsp chopped fresh
1 tsp curry powder	1 small eggplant, diced	coriander, to garnish
450 ml/¾ pt vegetable	3 garlic cloves, crushed	
stock	½ tsp chilli powder	
2 Tbsp vegetable oil	¼ tsp turmeric	
100 g/4 oz French beans	½ tsp ground cumin	
100 g/4 oz carrots, diced	½ tsp ground coriander	

Wash the lentils and place them in a large pan with the salt and curry powder. Add the stock and soak for 15 minutes. Bring to the boil, reduce the heat, cover and simmer for 15 minutes. Turn off the heat and leave to stand another 5 minutes.

Meanwhile, heat the oil in a frying pan, add the vegetables, garlic, spices and soy sauce and stir-fry for 10 minutes. Switch off the heat and leave to cool. Mix the lentils and vegetables, sprinkle with chopped coriander. Serve.

Spinach Noodle Salad

Young spinach leaves should be used for this recipe. The small leaves taste and look terrific with the spicy sauce and noodles.

serves 4

225 g/8 oz flat rice noodles
2 Tbsp groundnut oil
8 spring onions, sliced
2 garlic cloves, crushed
½ tsp star anise, ground
2 tsp fresh root ginger

2 Tbsp dark soy sauce
75 g/3 oz young spinach leaves, washed
1 Tbsp sesame oil
2 Tbsp chopped fresh coriander, to garnish

Cook the noodles in boiling water for 4 to 5 minutes. Drain and cool in cold water. Heat the groundnut oil in a wok and cook half of the spring onions, garlic, star anise, ginger and soy sauce for 2 minutes, stirring often. Cool completely.

Arrange the spinach in a serving bowl. Drain the noodles and toss into the vegetables. Sprinkle over the sesame oil and place on top of the spinach. Sprinkle with remaining spring onions and serve garnished with fresh coriander.

Sweet and Sour Vegetables

These vegetables have quite a strongly flavoured sauce and should be served
with plainer meats, fish or poultry.

serves 4	
I Tbsp olive oil	50 g/2 oz beansprouts
225 g/8 oz broccoli	100 g/4 oz mushrooms,
flowerets	sliced
½ red onion, thinly	2 Tbsp honey
sliced	2.5 cm/I in piece root
2 courgettes, sliced	ginger, grated
I carrot, cut into	2 Tbsp light soy sauce
thin strips	2 Tbsp cider vinegar

Heat the oil in a large wok or frying pan, and fry the broccoli for
3 minutes. Stir in the onion, courgettes and carrot and cook for a further
2 to 3 minutes. Add the beansprouts and mushrooms and stir-fry for
I minute.

Mix the honey, ginger, soy sauce and vinegar together. Pour into the pan,
stir and cook for 2 minutes. Serve immediately.

Green Peppers and Deep-fried Tofu

Quick to prepare, this recipe is best served immediately. If you can't find Chinese mushrooms use any large mushrooms as a substitute.

serves 4

for the sauce	for the dish
1 tsp potato flour	1 Tbsp groundnut or
5 Tbsp mushroom	corn oil
water	2 thin slices fresh root
2 Tbsp oyster sauce	ginger, peeled
2 tsp light soy sauce	4 large leaves Chinese
2 Tbsp vegetable oil	celery-cabbage,
1 garlic clove, finely	shredded
chopped	1 large green pepper,
2 spring onions, cut	seeded and diced
into small sections,	Oil for deep frying
white and green	250 g/9 oz packet tofu
parts separated	(soya beancurd),
4 large dried Chinese	dried and cut into
mushrooms, soaked,	rectangles
squeezed and cut	Salt
into thin strips	
(water to be	
reserved)	

First make the sauce. Mix the potato flour, mushroom water, oyster sauce and soy sauce. Heat a wok, add 2 tablespoons of oil and swirl around. Add the garlic, white spring onions and Chinese mushrooms. Stir for 30 seconds and pour into potato-flour mixture. Reduce heat and continue to stir until the sauce thickens. Remove from heat.

Heat 1 tablespoon of oil in a wok over high heat until smoking. Add the ginger, cabbage and green pepper. Toss for 30 seconds. Season, reduce heat and cook, covered, for 2 minutes. Remove and put into a large pan.

Half-fill the wok with oil, turn up heat to 100°C/200°F, and lower the tofu into the oil, one at a time. Fry for 4 minutes, turning over occasionally. Remove with a slotted spoon and drain on kitchen paper.

Lay the tofu on the cabbage in the pan and add the green spring onions. Heat the sauce and pour over the tofu. Heat for 2 minutes and serve.

Mangetout and Mushroom Stir-fry

This is a colourful nutritious vegetable dish that is quick to cook, and ideal
served with grilled meats and fish.

100 g/4 oz mangetout	100 g/4 oz broccoli	2 tsp light soy sauce
1 Tbsp olive oil	flowerets	1 garlic clove, crushed
100 g/4 oz baby corn	1 leek, sliced	2 tsp sesame seeds
cobs, cut lengthways	100 g/4 oz mushrooms	1 tsp sesame oil

Trim the mangetout. Heat the oil in a large frying pan or wok, and cook
the mangetout, corn, broccoli and leek for 5 minutes.

Stir in the sliced mushrooms, soy sauce, garlic and sesame seeds and cook
for 3 minutes. Add the sesame oil, stirring and serve.

Glazed Carrots

This is a very quick recipe for glazed carrots which are often baked in the oven.
Quite sweet to taste, they make a delicious accompaniment
to roast meats.

serves 4

450 g/1 lb baby carrots	2 tsp cornflour
Juice of 2 small oranges	Grated rind of 1 orange
2 Tbsp butter	1 Tbsp chopped fresh
2 tsp soft brown sugar	chives
2 tsp dark soy sauce	Ground black pepper

Cook the carrots in boiling water for 6 to 7 minutes. Meanwhile, mix the
orange juice, butter, sugar, soy sauce, orange rind and chives in a pan.

Blend the cornflour with 4 teaspoons of cold water and add to the pan.
Bring to the boil, stirring until thickened. Drain the carrots. Place in a
serving dish, pour over the sauce and serve.

Vegetable Spring Rolls

These spring rolls are ideal as part of a Chinese meal. Soy sauce gives the
vegetables an extra special flavour.

makes 20 rolls

225 g/8 oz fresh	Oil for deep-frying	filo pastry, defrosted
beansprouts	1½ tsp salt	if frozen
225 g/8 oz young tender	1 tsp sugar	
leeks or spring onions	1 Tbsp light soy sauce	
100 g/4 oz carrots	1 packet of 20 spring	
100 g/4 oz mushrooms	roll pastry squares or	

Wash and rinse the beansprouts and drain them thoroughly. Cut the
leeks or spring onions, carrots and mushrooms into thin shreds. Heat 3 to
4 tablespoons of oil in a wok or frying pan and stir-fry all the vegetables
for a few seconds. Add the salt, sugar and soy sauce and continue stirring
for 1 to 1½ minutes. Remove and leave to cool a little.

To cook the spring rolls, heat about 6 cups of oil in a wok until it starts
to smoke. Reduce the heat for a few minutes to cool the oil a little
before adding the spring rolls. Deep fry 6 to 8 at a time, 3 to 4 minutes
or until golden and crispy. Increase the heat to high again before frying
each batch. As each batch is cooked, remove and drain on kitchen paper.
Serve hot immediately.

Mushroom Pilaf

Mushroom pilaf is tasty enough to be served alone as a side dish. Or, use it as a base for serving stir-fried entrées.

serves 4		
2 tsp butter	375 g/6 oz brown rice	2 Tbsp Parmesan
100 g/4 oz mushrooms	250 ml/8 fl oz rosé wine	cheese, grated
1 onion, chopped	250 ml/8 fl oz chicken	
1 garlic clove, crushed	stock	
½ tsp salt	1 Tbsp light soy sauce	

Heat the butter in a pan and cook the sliced mushrooms, the onions and garlic until soft but not browned. Add the salt and rice and fry for 5 minutes. Stir in the wine, chicken stock and soy sauce.

Cover and simmer until the rice is cooked, adding more liquid as necessary. When the rice is ready, stir in the cheese.

Broad Bean and Walnut Casserole

Broad beans and walnuts are a great combination, especially when cooked in a mustard sauce and topped with melting cheese.

serves 4

450 g/1 lb broad beans, shelled	2 tsp wholegrain mustard
½ tsp salt	2 Tbsp light soy sauce
2 Tbsp butter	100 g/4 oz walnut pieces
1 onion, cut into 16 pieces	Salt and ground black pepper
1 garlic clove, crushed	50 g/2 oz Cheddar cheese, grated
½ tsp curry powder	
5 Tbsp vegetable stock	

Heat the oven to 180°C/350°F/Gas mark 4. Cook the beans in boiling salted water for 5 minutes. Drain well. Meanwhile, melt the butter in a frying pan or wok and cook the onion, garlic and curry powder for 5 minutes until softened. Stir in the stock, mustard, soy sauce, walnuts, seasoning and drained beans.

Transfer the mixture to a shallow ovenproof dish and sprinkle with cheese. Bake until the cheese has melted, about 30 minutes. Serve at once.

Steamed Mixed Vegetables

Steaming is one of the healthiest and tastiest methods of cooking vegetables.

serves 4

100 g/4 oz cauliflower flowerets	75 g/3 oz asparagus spears, trimmed
50 g/2 oz mangetout	1 orange pepper, quartered and cut into thin strips
50 g/2 oz chestnut mushrooms, quartered	2 Tbsp light soy sauce
1 red onion, cut into 8 pieces	1 tsp fish sauce
50 g/2 oz canned bamboo shoots, drained	1 tsp dried lemon grass
	4 tsp lemon juice
	2 tsp fennel seeds

Cut 4 large squares of baking parchment. Divide the vegetables equally between the paper and scrunch the paper together to form a parcel.

Mix the soy sauce, fish sauce, lemon grass, lemon juice and fennel seeds. Spoon the mixture onto the vegetables and seal the parcels firmly. Cook in a steamer until the vegetables are tender, 20 minutes.

Deep-fried Mushrooms

Using different varieties of wild and cultivated mushrooms makes this dish very attractive. If possible, marinate the mushrooms for up to 5 hours for a really strong flavour.

serves 4

100 g/4 oz oyster mushrooms	2 Tbsp dark soy sauce
100 g/4 oz shiitake mushrooms	2 Tbsp chopped fresh chives
100 g/4 oz open-cap mushrooms, peeled and halved	25 g/1 oz plain flour
150 ml/¼ pt red wine, such as burgundy	for the batter
2 garlic cloves, crushed	1 egg
3 Tbsp red wine vinegar	150 ml/¼ pt water
	100 g/4 oz plain flour
	1 Tbsp Parmesan cheese, grated
	Oil for deep-frying

Place all the mushrooms in a shallow dish. Mix the wine, garlic, red wine vinegar, soy sauce, chives and flour together. Pour over the mushrooms, cover and marinate for 2 hours.

Beat the egg and water for the batter together. Sieve the flour into a bowl and stir in the cheese. Make a well in the centre and gradually beat in the egg mix to form a smooth batter. Heat the oil in a wok to 190°C/375°F.

Remove the mushrooms from the marinade and roll in the flour. Dip into the batter to coat. Deep fry until golden, 3 minutes. Drain and pat dry with kitchen paper. Sprinkle with Parmesan cheese and serve.

Courgette and Sweet Potato Casserole

The colours of the courgette and sweet potato make this very visually pleasing. The vegetables are baked in soured cream and topped with melting mozzarella cheese.

serves 4

450 g/1 lb sweet potato, sliced	300 ml/½ pt soured cream	Salt and ground black pepper
450 g/1 lb courgette, sliced	½ tsp ground allspice	50 g/2 oz Mozzarella cheese, sliced
1 leek, sliced	1 Tbsp light soy sauce	
	1 Tbsp fresh thyme	

Cook the sweet potato, courgette and leek in a pan of boiling water for 15 minutes. Drain well. Preheat the oven to 170°C/325°F/Gas mark 3. Arrange the courgette, potato and leek in a shallow ovenproof dish. Mix the soured cream, allspice, soy sauce and thyme together. Pour over the vegetables and season well with the salt and pepper.

Place the cheese on top of the vegetables. Bake until golden, 30 minutes.

Spicy Beans

These beans have a rich caramel flavour due to the treacle and brown sugar. They are quite filling and almost a meal in themselves.

serves 4

225 g/8 oz dried beans, soaked overnight	2 Tbsp tomato purée
1 tsp salt	400 g/14 oz can chopped tomatoes
1 onion, halved and sliced	2 Tbsp soft brown sugar
1 green pepper, cut into strips	1 Tbsp treacle
100 g/4 oz cooked smoked ham, diced	2 Tbsp dark soy sauce
100 g/4 oz sliced spicy sausage, sliced	150 ml/¼ pt vegetable stock
	1 Tbsp cider vinegar
	1 green chilli, chopped
	1 tsp paprika

Drain and rinse the beans, then place them in a pan of salted water. Bring to the boil and boil rapidly for 10 minutes. Remove any foam with a slotted spoon. Drain well. Heat the oven to 180°C/350°F/Gas mark 4. Place the beans in a casserole dish. Add the onion, pepper, ham and sausage. Mix the tomato purée, tomatoes, brown sugar, molasses, soy sauce, stock, vinegar, chilli and paprika. Pour over the bean mix, stir and cover. Cook in the oven for 50 minutes.

Sweet Potato Muffins

These sweet, moist muffins are good either plain or served with honey.

makes about 12	
450 g/1 lb sweet potatoes, cooked, peeled and mashed	2 eggs
	1 Tbsp baking powder
	1 Tbsp light soy sauce
50 g/2 oz butter	60 ml/2 fl oz milk
50 g/2 oz brown sugar	175 g/6 oz plain flour

Boil the sweet potato in a pan of water until soft, about 20 minutes. Peel and mash. Heat the oven to 190°C/375°F/Gas mark 5. Cream the butter and brown sugar together. Add the mashed sweet potato, eggs, baking powder and soy sauce. Finally, stir in the milk and flour and mix thoroughly.

Stir-fried Courgette with Sesame Seeds

Soy sauce brings out the flavour of courgettes and the sesame seeds add crunch.

serves 4	
4 large courgettes, sliced	4 tsp light soy sauce
	½ tsp dill weed
2 tsp olive oil	2 tsp sesame seeds

Wash the courgette and slice into 3 to 5 mm/⅛- to ¼-in rounds. Heat the oil in a pan over medium heat and add the zucchini. Sprinkle the soy sauce and dill weed over the top and fry for 4 minutes until the courgettes begins to wilt. Add the sesame seeds and continue cooking until the courgettes starts to brown, about 4 minutes. Serve immediately.